ASK ISAAC ASIMOV

IS OUR PLANET WARMING UP?

BY ISAAC ASIMOV

Gareth Stevens Children's Books
MILWAUKEE

For a free color catalog describing Gareth Stevens' list of high-quality children's books, call 1-800-341-3569 (USA) or 1-800-461-9120 (Canada).

Library of Congress Cataloging-in-Publication Data

Asimov, Isaac, 1920-
    Is our planet warming up? / by Isaac Asimov.
       p. cm. — (Ask Isaac Asimov)
    Includes bibliographical references and index.
    Summary: Examines the problem of global warming, its possible causes, and ways to
prevent the situation from getting worse.
    ISBN 0-8368-0744-8
    1. Global warming—Juvenile literature. 2. Climatic changes—Juvenile literature. [1.
Global warming.] I. Title. II. Series: Asimov, Isaac, 1920-   Ask Isaac Asimov.
QC981.8.G56A84 1991
363.73'87—dc20   91-50359

A Gareth Stevens Children's Books edition

Edited, designed, and produced by
Gareth Stevens Children's Books
1555 North RiverCenter Drive, Suite 201
Milwaukee, Wisconsin 53212, USA

Picture Credits
pp. 2-3, courtesy of NASA; pp. 4-5, © Bryan and Cherry Alexander; pp. 6-7, Pat Ortega, 1991; pp. 8-9, © Ken Wardius/Third Coast; pp. 10-11, Mark Mille/DeWalt and Associates, 1991; pp. 12-13, Michael Medynsky/Artisan, 1991; p. 12 (inset), Mark Mille/DeWalt and Associates, 1991; pp. 14-15, © Mark Edwards/Still Pictures; pp. 16-17, © Chico Paulo/Third Coast; pp. 18-19, © D. Houston/Bruce Coleman Limited; pp. 20-21, © Mark Edwards/Still Pictures; pp. 22-23, © 1992 Greg Vaughn; p. 24, © 1992 Greg Vaughn

Cover photograph, © Bruce Davidson/Survival Anglia: The desert Sun bakes the land in Tsavo East National Park in Kenya. Because of extra carbon dioxide and methane in our atmosphere, the entire planet may be warming up.

Series editor: Elizabeth Kaplan
Series designer: Sabine Beaupré
Picture researcher: Diane Laska
Consulting editor: Matthew Groshek

Printed in MEXICO

2 3 4 5 6 7 8 9 98 97 96 95 94 93 92

Contents

Words that appear in the glossary are printed in **boldface** type the first time they occur in the text.

Exploring Our Environment

Look around you. You see deserts, forests, lakes, and rivers. You see farms, factories, houses, and cities. All of these things make up our **environment**. Sometimes there are problems with the environment. For instance, the Earth's climate may be warming up more quickly than it ever has in the past. Rapid **global warming** could cause severe problems for all living things on our planet. Why is this warming trend occurring? Let's find out.

Natural Changes in Climate

In times past, the Earth's **climate** was very different from our climate today. For example, millions of years ago, when dinosaurs roamed the Earth, our planet was warmer than it is today. In contrast, only a few thousand years ago, the climate was colder than today's climate. Huge sheets of ice, or **glaciers**, covered large parts of the Earth.

Such changes in climate are natural. They take place over thousands of years. Animals, plants, and people can usually adjust to these slow changes.

Quick Warm-up

Today the Earth's climate seems to be warming up much more quickly than it ever has in the past. Since the late 1800s, the Earth's average temperature seems to have risen almost 1°F (0.5°C). Some scientists predict that the average temperature may rise 3°F (1.5°C) in the next fifty years.

Even a temperature rise of one degree in a few centuries is difficult for most plants and animals to adjust to. A jump of three degrees in half a century may kill off many living things. Many plants and animals may die out, or become **extinct**.

Holding in the Heat

To understand why the Earth is warming up,
you need to understand why it is warm in
the first place. Our planet is surrounded by
a thick layer of gases called the **atmosphere**.
Sunlight passes through the atmosphere and
strikes the Earth. The Sun's rays heat up the
Earth's surface. The heat rises into the air.
Some of the gases in the atmosphere,
including **carbon dioxide** and **methane**, trap
the heat and reflect it back to Earth. This
keeps our planet warm.

In and Out of the Greenhouse

The process by which Earth's atmosphere holds in heat is known as the **greenhouse effect**. Like the glass that forms a greenhouse, the gases in the atmosphere let sunlight through. And like the panes of glass, the carbon dioxide and methane in the atmosphere hold in the heat.

Without these greenhouse gases, the Earth would be a cold, hostile place. The average temperature would drop below freezing. Life as we know it could not exist.

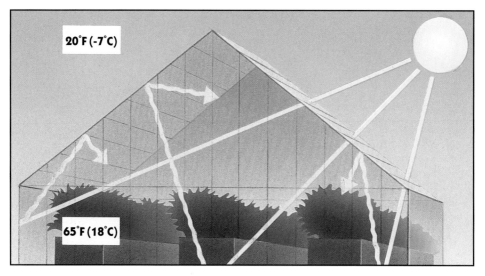

20°F (-7°C)

65°F (18°C)

How a greenhouse holds in heat.

Too Much of a Good Thing

Greenhouse gases in small quantities are a good thing. But in recent years, the amounts of carbon dioxide and methane released into our atmosphere have increased greatly. The Earth absorbs some of these gases naturally. Still, the levels of greenhouse gases in the atmosphere are on the rise. Many people are afraid that the extra greenhouse gases will turn our planet into an uncomfortable hot-house, where living things will have to hide from the Sun's searing heat.

The Root of the Problem

The extra carbon dioxide and methane in our atmosphere have one main source: us. When we burn **fossil fuels** — coal, oil, and natural gas — we release these gases into the air.

Clearing and burning forests also increases the greenhouse gases in the atmosphere. Trees take in, or absorb, carbon dioxide from the air and combine it with water to make food for themselves. When large forests are cut down, there are fewer trees to absorb carbon dioxide. So levels of this gas go up.

16

Crisis — Now or Never?

Although levels of greenhouse gases are rising, scientists disagree about how this will affect our climate. Some scientists think the Earth isn't warming up rapidly and that we and other living things will be able to adjust.

Other scientists think that a rapid warming trend is upon us and that we are heading for a global crisis. They think that the world's farms will turn into deserts, and lakes and rivers will dry up. They predict melting glaciers will raise the levels of the oceans, flooding the great coastal cities of the world.

19

What Can You Do?

Power plants and cars release tons of greenhouse gases every day. So you can help halt global warming by using less electricity and by finding ways to get around besides in a car. Ride a bicycle or walk rather than going by car. Turn off lights when you leave a room. Ask your parents to turn down the heat or air conditioning to **conserve** energy.

Another way to help halt global warming is to plant and care for trees. Because trees take in carbon dioxide, they are our natural allies in the fight against global warming.

Looking to the Future

The problem of global warming can't be solved in a day. It may take a long time to find clean sources of energy, such as wind energy, to replace fossil fuels. It may take a long time to replant the trees we are cutting down. But every little thing each person can do to conserve energy and to save our forests will help. Think about our planet. Think about ways you can help make the Earth a safe and comfortable place for the future.

More Books to Read

Global Warming: Assessing the Greenhouse Threat by Laurence
    Pringle (Arcade Publications)
The Global Warming Threat by Judith Woodburn (Gareth Stevens)
The Greenhouse Effect by Jack Harris (Crestwood House)

Places to Write

Here are some places you can write to for more information about
global warming and what you can do to help prevent it. Be sure to
tell them exactly what you want to know about. Give them your
full name and address so that they can write back to you.

The Alliance to Save Energy
1725 K Street NW
Suite 914
Washington, D.C. 20006

Environment Canada
Inquiry Center
351 St. Joseph Boulevard
Hull, Quebec   K1A 0H3

Climate Institute
324 Fourth Street NE
Washington, D.C. 20003

National Center for
    Atmospheric Research
Information and Education
    Outreach Program
P.O. Box 3000
Boulder, Colorado 80307-3000

Glossary

atmosphere (AT-muh-sfear): the gases that surround the Earth.

carbon dioxide: a gas in the Earth's atmosphere that contains one
    atom of carbon and two atoms of oxygen; carbon dioxide helps
    trap heat near the Earth's surface.

climate (KLIE-miht): the average or normal weather that a place
    has over a long period of time.

conserve (cuhn-SERV): to save; to conserve energy means to save energy by using less of it.

environment (en-VIE-run-ment): the natural and artificial things that make up the Earth.

extinct (eks-TINKT): no longer existing.

fossil fuels: coal, oil, and natural gas; these fuels formed from decaying plant and animal remains that were buried beneath the Earth's surface millions of years ago.

glaciers (GLAY-shurz): huge sheets of ice that once covered much of the Earth's surface; today glaciers are found in polar regions and near the tops of mountains.

global warming: the rapid warming trend that the Earth may be undergoing due to increased levels of carbon dioxide, methane, and other gases in the atmosphere.

greenhouse effect: the process by which carbon dioxide, methane, and other gases in the atmosphere trap heat close to the Earth, much as glass in a greenhouse traps heat inside the building.

methane (METH-ayn): a gas in the Earth's atmosphere made up of one carbon atom and four hydrogen atoms; methane helps trap heat near the Earth's surface.

Index